Broken Time

Broken Time

poems
by

John Mark Eberhart

THE MID–AMERICA PRESS, INC.
Warrensburg, Missouri 64093–0575

**Missouri Center
for the Book**

ë8.ë8.ë8.

**Missouri Authors
Collection**

ISBN 978-0910479-43-1

For John Fitzgerald Johnson and his sons,
lovers of music,
and for Sam and Deanna Eberhart,
my blood

CONTENTS

II. Lyrics

ACKNOWLEDGEMENTS

Cover design: Neil Nakahodo.
First reading of manuscript: My wife, Sherri Eberhart.
First edit: Kathleen Johnson.
Final edit: Robert C. Jones (The Doc!).
Technical advice on matters musical: My brother,
Ken Eberhart.
Copy editing: Paula Southerland.

I also wish to thank David Anstaett and Bill Bauer
for their encouragement of my work.

Several of the poems in this collection appeared in
publications as follows:
"Broken Time" and "Farmers" in *Coal City Review*
"Shadowboxing" in *The I-70 Review*
"North Dakota" and "Stranded" in *The Kansas City
Star*
"She Claims the Moon" in *The Mid-America Poetry
Review*
"Pat Metheny" in *The Midwest Quarterly*
"The Gospel of the Dirt" in *New Letters*
"Winter Garden" in *Pleiades*
"Ruts" and "Saints and Witches" in *The Same*
"Bonnie Raitt" in *Yellow Mustard*

Broken time: a way of playing in which the beat is not stated explicitly. Irregular, improvised syncopation.

—The Jazz Piano Study Letter

I. MUSIC

Broken Time

The couch, cigarette-scarred.
The ivy is taking the windows.
A flickering bulb, an empty
stein, a scattering of ashes.
But the music plays on, slow
jazz, counterpoint to the war
on the silent TV. The cannabis
burns, the beer goes down.

I'm going to get up in a while.
I'm going to clean this house
from end to end. I'm going
to get zealous tomorrow.
Tomorrow, it's rock 'n' roll.
Brooms, mops, bass drums.
Give me a backbeat and
I can conquer the world.

But this is the night, the time
for broken time. The bassist
lays out. The drummer loses
the beat. A piano note
lingers, curls into smoke.
I look at the clock as the
second-hand sticks—and you
bare your neck for a kiss.

North Dakota

Town was ten miles away.
Each morning at three,
the coyotes' jamboree.
The hoot owls at four.
At five, Orion overhead
as I unzipped the tent door
and tried to make coffee,
sunrise yet three hours
away. Ice in the fire ring,
full moon on the ridge.
A new moon in my mind:
You, seven hundred miles
south, waiting, like me,
for the light.

Panhandle

first pluck of the string
last rays of the prairie sun
music turns the sphere

The Muse

is petulant
when you leave her
with all your scribbled lines
and go out for blues and tequila.

Bonnie Raitt

She has this new album out,
real good stuff, glass slides
on steel strings, but I can't
focus on her lyrics, because
I keep looking at the CD cover.
She's decked out in red hair
with that shock of white,
and all I want to do is take
the guitar out of her hands
and tell her every sweet
blue lie I can conjure.

Charles Ives

They called him the Yankee maverick.
He was a tree, falling into his
own musical forest, but it didn't
vex him that no one might ever hear.
Some still don't. In Kansas City, in our
cracked and broken symphony hall,
a man in a plaid sportscoat and

a comb-over stands and says in a voice
loud as his attire: "What a crock."
Laughing at his coda, his companions
follow him out the door. They won't
return from the intermission. It isn't
even one of the tough ones; it's
the "Camp Meeting," the Third,

and it brought Ives the Pulitzer Prize.
Fifty damned years since he died;
the knuckleheads are still on his
case. The brass bands, the broken
time signatures, the noises from
nowhere: Few want these things.
Which just makes the din sweeter.

Blind Willie Johnson

All the other bluesmen played the bars,
but Blind Willie played in church instead.
Both places fed the hungry faces of the blues.
At the tavern and the altar, the women sang along.

Willie couldn't keep good time; his rhythms ran
like children playing in the dark down by the creek.
His singing voice was loud and low and froggy.
When my first wife left, she left his records with me.

I used to fight with that woman over Willie.
I'd call him a genius and she'd call me a fool.
I'd turn down the lights to get her in the mood.
She'd turn up the TV and flip the bird at me.

I've got a new wife but I want my old one back,
just for one night so I can prove myself right.
I'd get her in my car and buckle her up tight.
I'd turn up the radio and here's what I'd say:

"Let's go to Texas and dig up Blind Willie's bones;
give him a guitar and see if he still has the blues.
I don't mean to be bitter but you need to reconsider.
Let's go to Texas; hear the preacher play the blues."

Chuck Berry

We're the pickup band.
Chuck Berry roams the stage,
duckwalks, spots a woman
in the front row and sings
"My Ding-A-Ling" to her;
we try to follow along.
Today, even the drummer can't
grab Chuck's riffs. The boss
is strung out on something—
God knows what, but we don't.

The song staggers into
its final bar. Chuck turns,
snarls, "Bastards!"
Mothers in the crowd start
walking out, babies crying
on their hips. We stand ashamed,
waiting to see if Chuck's epithet
constitutes today's coda.
But he calls out, "Maybelline,"
and we're even worse on this one.
Chuck glares at us, faces the crowd again.

It's going to be a long day.

But if we were jazz musicians,
they'd say we were brilliant.

Ornette Coleman

"The Riddle," he calls it.
Good call, Mr. Coleman.
I'm listening, trying hard,
telling myself I'm not stupid.

But here I am again, looking
for a groove. Maybe there's
no shame in guesswork.
Sometimes it's good to get lost.

Pat Metheny

Who knew so much jazz
lay coiled in this wild-haired kid
with the big hayseed grin?
Maybe it was the storm clouds,
bearing down on Lee's Summit
all the way from Wichita,
that made him dig his nails
into that first guitar and
thunder back at the sky.

When Dylan Went Electric

Yasgur's Farm was still just a field
and tie-dyed trousers weren't trendy
and the Kennedys weren't dead or bloated
and the moon wasn't littered with metal
and the flood hadn't humbled us
and not all pop songs were 'product'
and the flag was stained but not soaked in blood.

Oaters

They're always best when they begin,
when the music comes over the mountains,
in those first few moments or scenes
where the composer trumps the director:
Elmer Bernstein making the orchestra
well up with doomed bravado for
"The Magnificent Seven," Ennio Morricone
getting wicked for Eastwood's "Man With
No Name"—even Mel Brooks' goofball songs
for Mongo and the "Blazing Saddles" fools.

Each first reel is like your life,
like getting up in the morning—
anything could happen; you could
get fired or get shot or get laid.

Once the action really starts,
it's almost always the same.
The pink slip or the orgasm
or the bullet in your belly;
you can't remember, at times
like those, to keep the music
pulsing away in your brain.

The outlaw rides into town.
The strings charge up, the trumpets
blare their useless warning,

the kettledrums pound down
the gunslinger's last rational thought
of good will or common sense.
Giddy-up! "Get the guy on the roof first!"
"Look out for the midget, the bad-hearted whore."
The whole town's keyed up, the sheriff's drunk,
and in the saloon, the fat-bottomed piano player
slams down his last chord and hides behind the bar,
driven to silence. They're waiting for *you*, waiting for
what you'll do. And you? You may have ten seconds
to live, but you're going to go out with a *bang.*

House on the Outskirts of Town

Something stands in the cornfield in the ghost heat.
Dust, summer sun, dreams ground down, death.
John keeps his father's guitar close at hand,
picks out pieces as Paul sings along. Mark plays
on the porch, watches the dog chase rabbits.
For them, time moves with the sun, morning to night.
For Mother, Grandmother, each day stands still.
In this old place, far out on the river road, they
sit behind shut doors, open books. They draw
the shades; no more need to look at the world.
Neighbors drive over. "Tell them, 'Not now,'"
Mother says, "not till we put things right around
here." The neighbors nod at the boys, go their way.

Inside, the women read their books—Dickens's
Christmas Carol, the early poems of Coleridge.
Grandmother stops talking. One day she wakes
from a doze, having dreamed of "Kubla Khan,"
and realizes the boys are grown and gone.
But she's happy. She has a secret. Lately
she's been hearing something new: The voice
a skeleton might have, clinking, rapping,
xylophone bones asking, "Where's my wife?"
She looks out the window at the cornfield.
She looks over at her daughter, white-haired now.
She says nothing. Opens her book again.
Smiles. Wets her finger. Turns another page.

Gort

Every time
the robot
comes out
of the ship
I think:
This time
maybe it
will be
different.
Every time
Bernard
Herrman's
music rises
behind the
metal man
I think:
*We humans
cannot really
be that bad.*

But the scene
is always
the same.

The Poet at 37,000 Feet

It's a fool's errand to try to write verse
when you're trapped on the airplane—
that antiseptic smell, those clean squalls
of air from the little nozzles in the panel.
I am not deceived; it reeks of death up here.
So of course I do it anyway: Take up the Bic
and start scratching. Most times, the results
are dreadful: clichéd little buggers—maybe
even haiku—spoiled before the ink's even dry.

Except this one. This one is giving me the willies.
This one is an engine shearing off into the blue.
This one is the young father standing twenty rows
in front of me, bouncing his infant son to sleep,
smiling because he does not know it's their last
day alive. This one is burning wreckage, severed
limbs, decapitation, bodies strewn over mountains.

But wait: I'm turning into William Shatner. I see
something out on the wing. I discover my window
will open. The death-air shrieks in, but I'm a rock.
I snatch these words from the page, fling them
out into the beyond, where they burst into flame,
destroy the wing-walking monster. I smell his
flesh burning, goatish, sacrificial and pure.

Rod Serling opens the cockpit door, resplendent
in his captain's bars, and walks down the aisle

18

to me. As he ambles, that twangy "Twilight Zone" music starts coming out of the overhead speakers: *"Doo doo doo doo, doo doo doo doo."* But all he says is, "Excellent work. You've saved us all." It's then I notice he's ignoring the "No Smoking" sign; there's that famous ciggy in his right hand.

But wait: It's really a joint. He offers; I take a puff. Next thing I know we're in the commercial break, selling Tide to housewives. "Oh, shit," I say. "I am so stoned." But Serling looks sharply at me. "That's next week's episode," he says. "Shirley Jackson's 'The Lottery.'"

Seth

Kansas City was a hot little town:
Gin halls, smoke, easy women.
Grandfather played the violin:
Ragtimes, dance tunes, jazz.
It was the only music in his life.

He sold my father to a sailor.
He traded my uncle to a whore.
He put my aunt in an orphanage.
He saved the worst for Grandma;
he locked her up in a nuthouse.

He named my other uncle after
himself—an act of hubris, of pure,
pointless narcissism; what kind
of man gives a son his name and
lets him grow up in a boys' home?

My father was five when he was
pawned for 50 bucks and some booze.
He never saw his brothers or sister
till they all had their own children.
They met, talked sibling sorrows.

But my father never saw his father again.
For my grandfather, my father would
always be five. Later on, there were letters,

Missouri to Michigan and back; the old
man had the nerve to call him "son."

The last letter was from his fourth wife.
I never saw it till I was nineteen. Found
it in a bond box under my parents' bed.
The old lady's tone was careful but
condescending, a dispatch to the distaff.

Seth—he'll never be Grandpa to me—
had put a bullet in his head. He'd been
working as a security guard. It proved
convenient, having the pistol around.
His final act: Gunning down the past.

Uncle Elvin

He told us kids something lived
in the old well, and we believed him.
"Listen," he'd say, and holler down.
When the echo came, he'd grin at us,
black eyes gleaming. "There he is."
"Who?" we'd ask. And Uncle Elvin
would laugh. "A fiddle player who
did too much fiddlin'. Don't get close!
He'll try to pull you down with his bow."
We grew up, gave up superstition.
But when Aunt Peg called last week
and told us how Uncle Elvin died,
the breath went right out of me.
She said he fell, but I wonder.

Drummer

They call him Mister Metronome;
he's never missed a beat.
It's when he hits the street
that things go wrong.

It's the whiskey bottle in his pocket.
It's the prostitutes he screws
before he goes home to his wife.
It's the lien on his van, the repo
man, the nights he fights, his
face split open on a barroom floor.

But mostly it's just too much timekeeping,
sitting in the back, on the riser, waiting
for the sneer from the saxman, who knows
this guy with the sticks has seen better days.

It's too much music but not enough time
to think about finding a better beat.

He exits, stage right, after the gig,
goes out the back door, and falls
all the way down the stairs, and dies,
a drunken paradiddle of a man.

Sunrise

The Baptists tried to save my soul.
Sunday mornings, Sunday evenings,
Wednesday night prayer meetings,
and—summers—vacation Bible school.

I was eager to go. There was a girl
there, when I was thirteen or so,
with a million starry freckles and
flaming hair like a red sun rising.

I would sit in the pew behind her,
mouthing hymns, mumbling prayers.
Now and then, she'd half-turn her
head, give me a glancing smile.

Thirty years later, I'm a deacon,
dozing through sermons, dreaming
of the flesh never conquered,
of the fire in that girl's eyes.

Sea of Glass

If this be triumph,
why are the harps out of tune?
Still waters. We wait.

Time Cubed

Each moment, some scientists
think, is as real as the next.
The steak you ate Sunday,
the hours you wasted watching
TV when you were ten,
the stroke that killed your
third-grade teacher just
as she was beginning
the math lesson—somewhere
in time's universe, all these
happenings are still happening.

If so, the past must be
squared by the future; we
just have to imagine it all:
the next note on the triangle,
the tree that will fall on your
house two summers hence,
the pop song that'll still
torment you in 25 years,
the way you'll stare at your
own hand on the coverlet
as you take your final breath.

But this is today, and it starts
with scalded coffee. An afternoon
downpour cancels your walk.
The book falls into your lap; the room

shimmers, then dims. Oh sure,
the *science* of it all may exist outside
the box, but here, we are ceilinged,
walled, floored. Ghosts whisper to us,
prophetic equations that root out our
fears, square up our hopes, dare us to
live in one past, one future, one present,

one exponential syllable: *Now.*

II. LYRICS

Ruts

The land rears up
out of the Blue River
and the cars on Red Bridge Road
snick past the little park
where the ruts are preserved.

I see no ghosts, but hear them:
The wagon masters, whips in hand.
"Faster!" they bellow, and the sun
races up the dirty trail
to burn down their lives.

The Funeral Director Takes a Poetry Class

I. Inhumation

Some days, I almost
look forward to it:
A silken, pillowed sleep,
no need to wake again

for work or play,
for rush hour,
airplanes, intercourse.

Above, a good, clean stone,
letters chiseled, indifferent
to the grinding wheel
of circumstance.

II. Exhumation

Being born is like being
unearthed. They reach in, pull
you out of that silken, pillowed
dark, give you a good once-over.

Will you be a
victim? Will you
be your own crime?

You spend a few thousand days
mulling it over, looking for
clues. Then it's epitaph time—
and someone else writes your ending.

Farmers

Out here in the fields,
the distances can
defeat you. In our
pickup trucks, we
raise the dust on
gravel roads, looking
for signs of trouble—
corn smut, busted fences,
a daughter in the hay.

Now and then you see us, you
city folks in your rental cars,
when you take a wrong turn
off the interstate and onto
one of our county roads
that have no names or
numbers, just letters—
G or B or double A.
The roads are like us;
they don't have much to say.

When we see you out here,
lost, your lips moving, your
eyes wide, looking for clues,
we'll wave to you—or at least
lift two fingers off the wheel.
If you stop and roll down your

window, we'll even give you
directions. We won't ask why
you're so quick to get away.
After all, you can't imagine
why we stay.

Rural School

When I hear the word *bucolic*,
it makes me want to fight.
This is what it was like:
A bootheel on your face.
Being forced to swallow spit.
Your head shoved into pig shit.
Your jockstrap over your eyes.
"Hey, asshole." "Hey, faggot."
"Hey, butthead." "Hey, fool."
Thirty years later, I still wake
sometimes, in dark of night,
from a dream in which I am
braining them all with a dictionary.

The Bitterroot Range

They say the mountains are beautiful
down in Colorado, but I've never been.
Up here, it's all lizards and twisted rock.
I've heard folks say, "Well, such and such
a place is the armpit of the world." This
must be the broken spine. Even our rivers
are sickly, ugly things. The Missouri starts
somewhere nearby, not at that state
park in Montana, but I've never been able
to find the spot. I'm busy anyhow. I've got
work to do. A few more wires to run, some
soldering, a weld here and there. I'm ready
for the fuse, the timer. From the far corner,
a rattlesnake watches me turn the screws.

Hooded Eagle Among Blinking Owls

Metaphysical, existential, melancholy:
Coleridge, with his visions of Xanadu,
of Cristabel, Mariner and albatross, was
something of a specter to the younger
Romantics. Gentle Shelley dubbed him
"hooded eagle among blinking owls."
One by one, the owls died as the eagle
lived on. Shelley, dead of drowning,
just shy of thirty years old. Keats
was younger yet, tuberculosis at
twenty-five. Byron, fevered in life,
was fevered in death, but he did
last a bit longer; he was thirty-six.
Only Wordsworth outlived Coleridge.
But that was no surprise. Unlike
the eagle, the old coot knew better
than to dip his beak in opium.

Departure

In boyhood I lived in the unmade world:
Open fields as mussed as my brother's
tousled head of hair, woods that tricked us
into circles, rainstorms that goaded
the creeks we knew into rivers, where we'd
tease the lizards, torment the water snakes.

How hateful now this world I've created:
The harsh geometries of this crowded room,
the knife-edged geography of the computer,
the straitjacket desk, the scattered scribbled
papers, work brought home from work—and
you, framed in the doorway, suitcase in hand.

Stranded

I see it this way:
The evening would be
coming on. Snow would
start making fenceposts
taller. Ice would sculpt
the trees into sentinels.
We'd hear reports of roads
being closed. I'd whisper
into your ear, " See, you
can't drive home tonight."
And all this white wrath—
winter woe for other folks—
would make both of us smile.

Falling

Snowflakes mock clock hands.
Ravens tell time with their wings.
Desire breaks the ice.

Fixer-Upper

I was OK when the basement
cracked, heaved in the drought,
and the dirty water poured in,
soaking rug and swelling floor.

I took it like a man when
the upstairs shower leaked
into the laundry room below,
made the plumber grin with greed.

When the burr oak bashed its way
through the dining-room skylight,
I just walked out to the garage,
got my chainsaw, started cutting.

The bedroom roof—now that did
try my patience. The ill-timed
thunderstorm, the water dripping
into my mouth, onto my lids.

But when you walked out that
crooked front door, cursing because
it wouldn't even slam behind you—it
was then I gave up on this eyesore.

In Retrospect

In retrospect, it doesn't
rain on your birthday party.
Your dad decides he loves
your mother after all.
Your track team takes
the state title and you're
the hero. You're the prom
king, the No. 1 draft pick,
employee of the month,
father of the year.

And none of your
lovers ever lies.

Remembrance

My brother
claims to recall
the contours of
the womb, the way
it felt to kick his
feet against the world.

He carries with him
a mental deposition
of my abuses: How
I smashed his toy cars,
shot him with a BB gun,
locked him in the cellar
on Halloween night.

I don't remember
such things at all.
But I'm sure
I'm guilty.

Winter Garden

After you left, I pulled
the last of the weeds,
swept the dry leaves
from the flagstones,
emptied the spent soil
from the big clay pots
and put them away
for the season.

Indoors now, I watch.
A mouse goes to ground
by the fieldstone wall;
the ghost owl misses
a meal. The white
ash, stripped bare
by the freeze, moans
like a witch in the wind.

Owls of North America

I. Northern Saw-Whet Owl

My voice is a saw,
scraping. The children's faces,
startled at my speech.

II. Snowy Owl

They steal the grasslands.
I would enjoy preying on
these human lemmings.

III. Common Barn Owl

Sparrow's blood freezes
as it hears the ghost owl scream,
exulting in dusk.

Mini Golf Course, Abandoned

People had fun here once. Young
couples on first dates, kids cutting
classes, old folks with those silly
plastic putters. Now the little fairways
are graveyard paths. Now the flagstones
whisper epitaphs. Late at night, two witches,
chanting spells, turn holes into cauldrons.
The earth vomits up golf balls, and the hags
hurl them at each other like old curses.

Batsuit

Jokers, riddlers
are waiting to wreck your workday,
to waste your time with
chuckles and yuks,
irksome questions:
"Make your quota this month?"

Christina, the catwoman,
purrs at the water cooler,
just like yesterday: "I don't
care about your wedding ring."

The boss is Mr. Freeze.
So's your salary.
So's your future.

Utility belt: Check.
Tights, gloves, bootstraps.
Don the cowl.
Don the cape.

Trudge in today;
trudge in tomorrow—
same bat time, same bat channel.

Twenty more years,
and you can hang it all up.

Croatoan

They were children to me,
these "colonists," these fools.
I eavesdropped on the prayers to their
God, laughed at their clumsy tools.

I wrote that word on the tree,
made sport of what they called life.
I put my finger to the bark, chuckled,
made my mark look like that of a knife.

While I slept, all these centuries,
I overheard your awed conjectures:
Indians burned them, drowned them.
Such are your intellectual specters.

I won't tell you what I did to them.
Someday, I'll do the same to you.

Shadowboxing

It is more myself
than I am. I wish
I were my shadow,
gliding, grounded,
good at secrets.

***

Look at him up there:
Risking a friendship,
arguing politics. Mute,
I gesture, matte hands
imploring: *Stop. Stop.*

Saints and Witches

The arrogance
of a blessing,
the madness
of a curse.

So we burn them
both at the stake
and let time
do its work.

Muscle Memory

I'm always awake by seven,
but my seven is seven at night.
I work those odd jobs—liquor
store clerk, night watchman at
a warehouse, the fellow who
bakes bread, stocks shelves.
I work each job till someone
wearies of my long jaw, my
sable eyes, then I move on.

Once, I sold a few paintings.
I called it the golden year;
it was as if I could taste
light's nectar, see colors
through the holes of my
ears. You were in every
canvas, hiding in parabolas,
scarifications, splatters
of paint, gouges in canvas.

I was trying to keep you
for myself. I masked your face
with bravura brushstrokes,
cupped your breasts in
abstract arcs, limned
your legs with chiaroscuro
hubris. Finally, you did

what I expected: You
took up with a sculptor.

Each morning, I get home
from work a bit before dawn.
I put down my keys, open the
blinds. I am trying to paint
ghosts. The brush moves like
a planchette; I am obeying
muscle memory. I am a thing
of tendon, of bone—of flesh
emptied of all but one craving:
to open myself to another day's light.

January

The nothingness after New Year's Day.
The shadows cast by the faithless sun.
The difficulty to do a thing, the voices
that say, "Slip away, sleep, slip away."

Yet at night, the hungry spirit roams,
trying to forage its way out of winter.
A truffle, the dregs of the egg nog,
one last stogy, "Twilight Zone" on TV.

She Claims the Moon

"It's ours," she says. "It pulls at our insides."
"But men went there," he says. She smiles.
"We didn't have to go. It's ours."

Sun, satellites, stars: reflections
of ripeness, fullness, birth.
She claims them all.

She laughs. "But men can have the
comets, with their looping paths,
lazy tails." He doesn't speak, but thinks:

*No, not even comets. Men are bound to earth,
to the mother, tugging at her for crops, coal,
gold, till she pulls us down into her forever.*

The Gospel of the Dirt

Darwin did believe in God,
or rather, could not quite let Him go.
Aboard the *Beagle*, his faith wavered,
rocked by the beauties of the sea.
If creatures no one ever saw could
be so lovely, what, then, of the logic
of the First Cause? The question
rankled. His daughter, Annie, died.
Forced to give her to the earth, he
compelled the Earth to give to him:
Fossils, barnacles, the tractable
stomachs of burrowing owls.
After *The Origin of Species* was

published, a journalist jeered that
Darwin's was the gospel of the dirt.
A cartoonist stole his solemn face,
mocked it, gave it the body of an ape.
Darwin lived; Darwin aged. His beard
turned white; near the end he looked
almost avuncular, a bowlered Jehovah.
In his follicles, cells divided, begat; in
his world as in ours, creatures unwitting
made their selections, lived in their own
scales, feathers, skins. Each molecule
its own Genesis; with every new day
above ground, Creation began.

Notes

"Chuck Berry" is based on a real concert I witnessed in Kansas City in the 1980s. For many years, it was Berry's habit to play with a "pickup band" of musicians he had never met, but who were supposed to know his songs. The results of this policy were not always optimal.

"Oaters" is a rather charming slang term for cowboy movies. They are best viewed very late at night.

"Gort" is the robot from the science fiction film "The Day the Earth Stood Still."

"The Bitterroot Range" was inspired by one of the most forbidding mountain ranges in the United States. I have been to this region of Idaho but have never built a bomb.

"Owls of North America" consists of three short poems that are part of a full-length manuscript I've completed called "The Ghost Owl's Lament." At this writing, I'm afraid, that book remains strictly for the birds.

"Mini Golf Course, Abandoned" was written while standing in front of a Mitch Epstein photo that was featured in "Where We Live: Photographs of America from the Berman Collection," which was displayed at Los Angeles' Getty Museum from Oct. 24, 2006, to Feb. 25, 2007.

"Croatoan" was the word found carved into a post on Roanoke Island off North Carolina in 1590 after the colony there—the first English settlement in America—disappeared. Some speculate that the intended message was that the colonists—more than 100 men, women and children—had moved to Croatoan Island, about fifty miles away. However, they were never found.

"Muscle Memory" is loosely based on the life of Willem de Kooning. I am indebted to Mark Stevens and Annalyn Swan, authors of "de Kooning: An American Master," for their excellent biography and their generosity in discussing it.

"The Gospel of the Dirt" is an actual phrase a journalist used to describe Charles Darwin's work. That was quite sometime ago now, though you would not know it by the comments one hears these days regarding evolution, religion and the like—and not just in Kansas, either.

Biography

John Mark Eberhart was born in St. Joseph, Missouri, in 1960. He earned a bachelor of journalism degree from the University of Missouri–Columbia in 1983 and a master's degree in English from the University of Missouri–Kansas City in 1998. In January 1987 he joined the staff of *The Kansas City Star,* and became the newspaper's book review editor in March 2000. His first poetry collection, *Night Watch,* was published by The Mid–America Press in June 2005. One poem from that collection, "Just One Ghost," was included in Helicon Nine's *Chance of a Ghost* anthology and also received Honorable Mention as one of the year's best poems in the Science Fiction Writers of America's anthology, *The Year's Best Fantasy and Horror 2006.* In 2006, UMKC honored him with its Alumni Award for the Arts and Sciences division.